A CHRISTIAN

Give thanks to the Lord

Want a freebie?!

Email us at
prettysimplebooks@gmail.com

Title the email "Give Thanks!" and
we'll send you something fun!

· ·

Visit our website
www.prettysimplebooks.com
And find us on Instagram
@prettysimplebooks

THIS BOOK BELONGS TO:

_____

_____

_____

— Give thanks to the Lord —

Rejoice always, pray continually, give thanks in all circumstances; for this is God's will for you in Christ Jesus.

1 Thessalonians 5:16–18

I AM THANKFUL FOR...   DATE: 8-27-2020

1. Family
2. Life
3. Love

I AM THANKFUL FOR...   DATE: 11/20/20   2:40

1. Skill
2. Education
3. Braveness

I AM THANKFUL FOR...   DATE:

1.
2.
3.

I AM THANKFUL FOR...   DATE:

1. _____
2. _____
3. _____

I AM THANKFUL FOR...   DATE:

1. _____
2. _____
3. _____

I AM THANKFUL FOR...   DATE:

1. _____
2. _____
3. _____

I AM THANKFUL FOR...   DATE:

1. _____
2. _____
3. _____

Prayer: _____

_____

Give thanks to the Lord

Give thanks to the LORD, for he is good; his love endures forever.

1 Chronicles 16:34

I AM THANKFUL FOR...   DATE:

1. _____
2. _____
3. _____

I AM THANKFUL FOR...   DATE:

1. _____
2. _____
3. _____

I AM THANKFUL FOR...   DATE:

1. _____
2. _____
3. _____

I AM THANKFUL FOR...   DATE:

1. _____
2. _____
3. _____

I AM THANKFUL FOR...   DATE:

1. _____
2. _____
3. _____

I AM THANKFUL FOR...   DATE:

1. _____
2. _____
3. _____

I AM THANKFUL FOR...   DATE:

1. _____
2. _____
3. _____

Prayer: _____

_____

Give thanks to the Lord

> Enter his gates with thanksgiving and his courts with praise; give thanks to him and praise his name. For the LORD is good and his love endures forever; his faithfulness continues through all generations.
>
> Psalm 100:4-5

I AM THANKFUL FOR...   DATE:

1. _____
2. _____
3. _____

I AM THANKFUL FOR...   DATE:

1. _____
2. _____
3. _____

I AM THANKFUL FOR...   DATE:

1. _____
2. _____
3. _____

I AM THANKFUL FOR...   DATE:

1. _____
2. _____
3. _____

I AM THANKFUL FOR...   DATE:

1. _____
2. _____
3. _____

I AM THANKFUL FOR...   DATE:

1. _____
2. _____
3. _____

I AM THANKFUL FOR...   DATE:

1. _____
2. _____
3. _____

Prayer: _____

_____

_____

Give thanks to the Lord

For this reason, ever since I heard about your faith in the Lord Jesus and your love for all God's people, I have not stopped giving thanks for you, remembering you in my prayers.

Ephesians 1:15-16

I AM THANKFUL FOR...   DATE:

1.
2.
3.

I AM THANKFUL FOR...   DATE:

1.
2.
3.

I AM THANKFUL FOR...   DATE:

1.
2.
3.

I AM THANKFUL FOR...   DATE:

1. _____
2. _____
3. _____

I AM THANKFUL FOR...   DATE:

1. _____
2. _____
3. _____

I AM THANKFUL FOR...   DATE:

1. _____
2. _____
3. _____

I AM THANKFUL FOR...   DATE:

1. _____
2. _____
3. _____

Prayer: _____
_____
_____

Give thanks to the Lord

Through Jesus, therefore, let us continually offer to God a sacrifice of praise—the fruit of lips that openly profess his name.

Hebrews 13:15

I AM THANKFUL FOR...   DATE:

1.
2.
3.

I AM THANKFUL FOR...   DATE:

1.
2.
3.

I AM THANKFUL FOR...   DATE:

1.
2.
3.

I AM THANKFUL FOR...   DATE:

1. _____
2. _____
3. _____

I AM THANKFUL FOR...   DATE:

1. _____
2. _____
3. _____

I AM THANKFUL FOR...   DATE:

1. _____
2. _____
3. _____

I AM THANKFUL FOR...   DATE:

1. _____
2. _____
3. _____

Prayer: _____

_____

Give thanks to the Lord

All this is for your benefit, so that the grace that is reaching more and more people may cause thanksgiving to overflow to the glory of God.

2 Corinthians 4:15

I AM THANKFUL FOR...   DATE:

1. _____
2. _____
3. _____

I AM THANKFUL FOR...   DATE:

1. _____
2. _____
3. _____

I AM THANKFUL FOR...   DATE:

1. _____
2. _____
3. _____

I AM THANKFUL FOR...   DATE:

1. _____
2. _____
3. _____

I AM THANKFUL FOR...   DATE:

1. _____
2. _____
3. _____

I AM THANKFUL FOR...   DATE:

1. _____
2. _____
3. _____

I AM THANKFUL FOR...   DATE:

1. _____
2. _____
3. _____

Prayer: _____
_____
_____

Give thanks to the Lord

Sing to the LORD with grateful praise; make music to our God on the harp.

Psalm 147:7

I AM THANKFUL FOR...   DATE:

1.
2.
3.

I AM THANKFUL FOR...   DATE:

1.
2.
3.

I AM THANKFUL FOR...   DATE:

1.
2.
3.

I AM THANKFUL FOR...   DATE:
....

1. _____
2. _____
3. _____

I AM THANKFUL FOR...   DATE:
....

1. _____
2. _____
3. _____

I AM THANKFUL FOR...   DATE:
....

1. _____
2. _____
3. _____

I AM THANKFUL FOR...   DATE:
....

1. _____
2. _____
3. _____

Prayer: _____
_____
_____

Give thanks to the Lord

> Let the peace of Christ rule in your hearts, since as members of one body you were called to peace. And be thankful.
>
> Colossians 3:15

I AM THANKFUL FOR...   DATE:

1. _____
2. _____
3. _____

I AM THANKFUL FOR...   DATE:

1. _____
2. _____
3. _____

I AM THANKFUL FOR...   DATE:

1. _____
2. _____
3. _____

I AM THANKFUL FOR...   DATE:
. . . .
1. _____
2. _____
3. _____

I AM THANKFUL FOR...   DATE:
. . . .
1. _____
2. _____
3. _____

I AM THANKFUL FOR...   DATE:
. . . .
1. _____
2. _____
3. _____

I AM THANKFUL FOR...   DATE:
. . . .
1. _____
2. _____
3. _____

Prayer: _____

_____

Give thanks to the Lord

First, I thank my God through Jesus Christ for all of you, because your faith is proclaimed in all the world.

Romans 1:8

I AM THANKFUL FOR...   DATE:

1.
2.
3.

I AM THANKFUL FOR...   DATE:

1.
2.
3.

I AM THANKFUL FOR...   DATE:

1.
2.
3.

I AM THANKFUL FOR...   DATE:

1. _____
2. _____
3. _____

I AM THANKFUL FOR...   DATE:

1. _____
2. _____
3. _____

I AM THANKFUL FOR...   DATE:

1. _____
2. _____
3. _____

I AM THANKFUL FOR...   DATE:

1. _____
2. _____
3. _____

Prayer: _____

_____

_____

Give thanks to the Lord

He is ever lending generously, and his children become a blessing.

Psalm 37:26

I AM THANKFUL FOR...   DATE:

1.
2.
3.

I AM THANKFUL FOR...   DATE:

1.
2.
3.

I AM THANKFUL FOR...   DATE:

1.
2.
3.

I AM THANKFUL FOR...   DATE:

1. _____
2. _____
3. _____

I AM THANKFUL FOR...   DATE:

1. _____
2. _____
3. _____

I AM THANKFUL FOR...   DATE:

1. _____
2. _____
3. _____

I AM THANKFUL FOR...   DATE:

1. _____
2. _____
3. _____

Prayer: _____
_____
_____

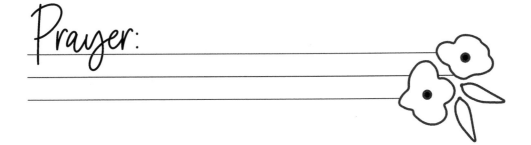

Give thanks to the Lord

We give thanks to you, Lord God Almighty, the One who is and who was, because you have taken your great power and have begun to reign.

Revelation 11:17

I AM THANKFUL FOR...   DATE:

1. _____
2. _____
3. _____

I AM THANKFUL FOR...   DATE:

1. _____
2. _____
3. _____

I AM THANKFUL FOR...   DATE:

1. _____
2. _____
3. _____

I AM THANKFUL FOR...   DATE:
. . . .

1.
2.
3.

I AM THANKFUL FOR...   DATE:
. . . .

1.
2.
3.

I AM THANKFUL FOR...   DATE:
. . . .

1.
2.
3.

I AM THANKFUL FOR...   DATE:
. . . .

1.
2.
3.

Prayer:

Give thanks to the Lord

I always thank my God for you because of his grace given you in Christ Jesus. For in him you have been enriched in every way—with all kinds of speech and with all knowledge.

1 Corinthians 1:4-5

I AM THANKFUL FOR...   DATE:

1. _____
2. _____
3. _____

I AM THANKFUL FOR...   DATE:

1. _____
2. _____
3. _____

I AM THANKFUL FOR...   DATE:

1. _____
2. _____
3. _____

I AM THANKFUL FOR...   DATE:
....

1. _____
2. _____
3. _____

I AM THANKFUL FOR...   DATE:
....

1. _____
2. _____
3. _____

I AM THANKFUL FOR...   DATE:
....

1. _____
2. _____
3. _____

I AM THANKFUL FOR...   DATE:
....

1. _____
2. _____
3. _____

Prayer: _____
_____
_____

Give thanks to the Lord

To you, O God of my fathers, I give thanks and praise, for you have given me wisdom and might, and have now made known to me what we asked of you, for you have made known to us the king's matter.

Daniel 2:23

I AM THANKFUL FOR...   DATE:

1. _____
2. _____
3. _____

I AM THANKFUL FOR...   DATE:

1. _____
2. _____
3. _____

I AM THANKFUL FOR...   DATE:

1. _____
2. _____
3. _____

I AM THANKFUL FOR...   DATE:

1. _____
2. _____
3. _____

I AM THANKFUL FOR...   DATE:

1. _____
2. _____
3. _____

I AM THANKFUL FOR...   DATE:

1. _____
2. _____
3. _____

I AM THANKFUL FOR...   DATE:

1. _____
2. _____
3. _____

Prayer: _____
_____
_____

there is always something
to be thankful for

Gratitude
CHECK IN

WHERE DID YOU SEE GOD TODAY? WRITE A NOTE OF
GRATITUDE THANKING GOD FOR BEING PRESENT IN YOUR
EVERY DAY.

_____
_____
_____
_____
_____
_____
_____
_____
_____
_____
_____
_____
_____
_____
_____
_____
_____
_____
_____
_____
_____
_____
_____
_____

Give thanks to the Lord

Praise the LORD. Give thanks to the LORD, for he is good; his love endures forever.

Psalm 106:1

I AM THANKFUL FOR...   DATE:

1. _____
2. _____
3. _____

I AM THANKFUL FOR...   DATE:

1. _____
2. _____
3. _____

I AM THANKFUL FOR...   DATE:

1. _____
2. _____
3. _____

I AM THANKFUL FOR...   DATE:
. . . .

1. _____
2. _____
3. _____

I AM THANKFUL FOR...   DATE:
. . . .

1. _____
2. _____
3. _____

I AM THANKFUL FOR...   DATE:
. . . .

1. _____
2. _____
3. _____

I AM THANKFUL FOR...   DATE:
. . . .

1. _____
2. _____
3. _____

Prayer: _____

_____

Give thanks to the Lord

Do not be anxious about anything, but in every situation, by prayer and petition, with thanksgiving, present your requests to God.

Philippians 4:6

I AM THANKFUL FOR...   DATE:

1. _____
2. _____
3. _____

I AM THANKFUL FOR...   DATE:

1. _____
2. _____
3. _____

I AM THANKFUL FOR...   DATE:

1. _____
2. _____
3. _____

I AM THANKFUL FOR...   DATE:

1. _____
2. _____
3. _____

I AM THANKFUL FOR...   DATE:

1. _____
2. _____
3. _____

I AM THANKFUL FOR...   DATE:

1. _____
2. _____
3. _____

I AM THANKFUL FOR...   DATE:

1. _____
2. _____
3. _____

Prayer: _____

_____

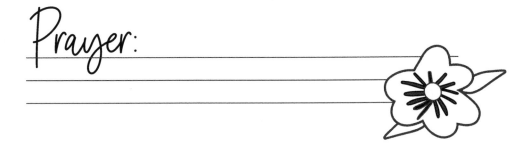

Give thanks to the Lord

This is the day that the Lord has made; let us rejoice and be glad in it.

Psalm 118:24

I AM THANKFUL FOR...　　　　　DATE:

1. _____

2. _____

3. _____

I AM THANKFUL FOR...　　　　　DATE:

1. _____

2. _____

3. _____

I AM THANKFUL FOR...　　　　　DATE:

1. _____

2. _____

3. _____

I AM THANKFUL FOR...   DATE:

1.
2.
3.

I AM THANKFUL FOR...   DATE:

1.
2.
3.

I AM THANKFUL FOR...   DATE:

1.
2.
3.

I AM THANKFUL FOR...   DATE:

1.
2.
3.

Prayer:

Give thanks to the Lord

> May mercy, peace, and love be multiplied to you.
>
> Jude 1:2

I AM THANKFUL FOR...   DATE:

1. _____
2. _____
3. _____

I AM THANKFUL FOR...   DATE:

1. _____
2. _____
3. _____

I AM THANKFUL FOR...   DATE:

1. _____
2. _____
3. _____

I AM THANKFUL FOR...   DATE:

1. _____
2. _____
3. _____

I AM THANKFUL FOR...   DATE:

1. _____
2. _____
3. _____

I AM THANKFUL FOR...   DATE:

1. _____
2. _____
3. _____

I AM THANKFUL FOR...   DATE:

1. _____
2. _____
3. _____

Prayer: _____

_____

Give thanks to the Lord

> Let them give thanks to the LORD for his unfailing love and his wonderful deeds for mankind, for he satisfies the thirsty and fills the hungry with good things.
>
> Psalm 107:8-9

I AM THANKFUL FOR...   DATE:

1. _____
2. _____
3. _____

I AM THANKFUL FOR...   DATE:

1. _____
2. _____
3. _____

I AM THANKFUL FOR...   DATE:

1. _____
2. _____
3. _____

I AM THANKFUL FOR...   DATE:

1. _____
2. _____
3. _____

I AM THANKFUL FOR...   DATE:

1. _____
2. _____
3. _____

I AM THANKFUL FOR...   DATE:

1. _____
2. _____
3. _____

I AM THANKFUL FOR...   DATE:

1. _____
2. _____
3. _____

Prayer: _____

_____

Give thanks to the Lord

And coming up at that very hour she began to give thanks to God and to speak of him to all who were waiting for the redemption of Jerusalem.

Luke 2:38

I AM THANKFUL FOR...   DATE:

1.
2.
3.

I AM THANKFUL FOR...   DATE:

1.
2.
3.

I AM THANKFUL FOR...   DATE:

1.
2.
3.

I AM THANKFUL FOR...   DATE:
....

1. _____
2. _____
3. _____

I AM THANKFUL FOR...   DATE:
....

1. _____
2. _____
3. _____

I AM THANKFUL FOR...   DATE:
....

1. _____
2. _____
3. _____

I AM THANKFUL FOR...   DATE:
....

1. _____
2. _____
3. _____

Prayer: _____
_____
_____

Give thanks to the Lord

The LORD is my strength and my shield; my heart trusts in him, and he helps me. My heart leaps for joy, and with my song I praise him.

Psalm 28:7

I AM THANKFUL FOR...   DATE:

1.
2.
3.

I AM THANKFUL FOR...   DATE:

1.
2.
3.

I AM THANKFUL FOR...   DATE:

1.
2.
3.

I AM THANKFUL FOR...   DATE:

1. _____
2. _____
3. _____

I AM THANKFUL FOR...   DATE:

1. _____
2. _____
3. _____

I AM THANKFUL FOR...   DATE:

1. _____
2. _____
3. _____

I AM THANKFUL FOR...   DATE:

1. _____
2. _____
3. _____

Prayer: _____

_____

Give thanks to the Lord

If I take part in the meal with thankfulness, why am I denounced because of something I thank God for? So whether you eat or drink or whatever you do, do it all for the glory of God.

1 Corinthians 10:30-31

I AM THANKFUL FOR...   DATE:

1. _____
2. _____
3. _____

I AM THANKFUL FOR...   DATE:

1. _____
2. _____
3. _____

I AM THANKFUL FOR...   DATE:

1. _____
2. _____
3. _____

I AM THANKFUL FOR...   DATE:

1. _____
2. _____
3. _____

I AM THANKFUL FOR...   DATE:

1. _____
2. _____
3. _____

I AM THANKFUL FOR...   DATE:

1. _____
2. _____
3. _____

I AM THANKFUL FOR...   DATE:

1. _____
2. _____
3. _____

Prayer: _____
_____
_____

Give thanks to the Lord

In every way and everywhere we accept this with all gratitude.

Acts 24:3

I AM THANKFUL FOR...   DATE:

1.
2.
3.

I AM THANKFUL FOR...   DATE:

1.
2.
3.

I AM THANKFUL FOR...   DATE:

1.
2.
3.

I AM THANKFUL FOR...   DATE:

1. _____
2. _____
3. _____

I AM THANKFUL FOR...   DATE:

1. _____
2. _____
3. _____

I AM THANKFUL FOR...   DATE:

1. _____
2. _____
3. _____

I AM THANKFUL FOR...   DATE:

1. _____
2. _____
3. _____

Prayer: _____
_____
_____

Give thanks to the Lord

Every good and perfect gift is from above, coming down from the Father of the heavenly lights, who does not change like shifting shadows.

James 1:17

I AM THANKFUL FOR...   DATE:

1. _____
2. _____
3. _____

I AM THANKFUL FOR...   DATE:

1. _____
2. _____
3. _____

I AM THANKFUL FOR...   DATE:

1. _____
2. _____
3. _____

I AM THANKFUL FOR...   DATE:

1. _____
2. _____
3. _____

I AM THANKFUL FOR...   DATE:

1. _____
2. _____
3. _____

I AM THANKFUL FOR...   DATE:

1. _____
2. _____
3. _____

I AM THANKFUL FOR...   DATE:

1. _____
2. _____
3. _____

Prayer: _____

_____

Give thanks to the Lord

I will give thanks to you, LORD, with all my heart; I will tell of all your wonderful deeds.

Psalm 9:1

I AM THANKFUL FOR...   DATE:

1.
2.
3.

I AM THANKFUL FOR...   DATE:

1.
2.
3.

I AM THANKFUL FOR...   DATE:

1.
2.
3.

I AM THANKFUL FOR...   DATE:
....

1. _____
2. _____
3. _____

I AM THANKFUL FOR...   DATE:
....

1. _____
2. _____
3. _____

I AM THANKFUL FOR...   DATE:
....

1. _____
2. _____
3. _____

I AM THANKFUL FOR...   DATE:
....

1. _____
2. _____
3. _____

Prayer: _____
_____
_____

Give thanks to the Lord

In that day you will say: "Give praise to the LORD, proclaim his name; make known among the nations what he has done, and proclaim that his name is exalted.

Isaiah 12:4

I AM THANKFUL FOR...   DATE:

1. _____
2. _____
3. _____

I AM THANKFUL FOR...   DATE:

1. _____
2. _____
3. _____

I AM THANKFUL FOR...   DATE:

1. _____
2. _____
3. _____

I AM THANKFUL FOR...   DATE:
....

1. _____
2. _____
3. _____

I AM THANKFUL FOR...   DATE:
....

1. _____
2. _____
3. _____

I AM THANKFUL FOR...   DATE:
....

1. _____
2. _____
3. _____

I AM THANKFUL FOR...   DATE:
....

1. _____
2. _____
3. _____

Prayer: _____

_____

_____

Give thanks to the Lord

> Therefore, since we are receiving a kingdom that cannot be shaken, let us be thankful, and so worship God acceptably with reverence and awe.
>
> Hebrews 12:28

I AM THANKFUL FOR...   DATE:

1. _____
2. _____
3. _____

I AM THANKFUL FOR...   DATE:

1. _____
2. _____
3. _____

I AM THANKFUL FOR...   DATE:

1. _____
2. _____
3. _____

I AM THANKFUL FOR...   DATE:

1. _____
2. _____
3. _____

I AM THANKFUL FOR...   DATE:

1. _____
2. _____
3. _____

I AM THANKFUL FOR...   DATE:

1. _____
2. _____
3. _____

I AM THANKFUL FOR...   DATE:

1. _____
2. _____
3. _____

Prayer: _____

_____

count your blessings

Gratitude
CHECK IN

LIST OUT THOSE BLESSINGS! WRITE A NOTE OF GRATITUDE
THANKING GOD FOR EVERY BLESSING IN YOUR LIFE.

_____

_____

_____

_____

_____

_____

_____

_____

_____

_____

_____

_____

_____

_____

_____

_____

_____

_____

_____

_____

_____

_____

_____

_____

_____

Give thanks to the Lord

> I will give thanks to the LORD because of his righteousness; I will sing the praises of the name of the LORD Most High.
>
> Psalm 7:17

I AM THANKFUL FOR...   DATE:

1. _____
2. _____
3. _____

I AM THANKFUL FOR...   DATE:

1. _____
2. _____
3. _____

I AM THANKFUL FOR...   DATE:

1. _____
2. _____
3. _____

I AM THANKFUL FOR...   DATE:

1. _____
2. _____
3. _____

I AM THANKFUL FOR...   DATE:

1. _____
2. _____
3. _____

I AM THANKFUL FOR...   DATE:

1. _____
2. _____
3. _____

I AM THANKFUL FOR...   DATE:

1. _____
2. _____
3. _____

Prayer:
_____
_____

Give thanks to the Lord

For where your treasure is, there your heart will be also.

Matthew 6:21

I AM THANKFUL FOR...   DATE:

1. _____
2. _____
3. _____

I AM THANKFUL FOR...   DATE:

1. _____
2. _____
3. _____

I AM THANKFUL FOR...   DATE:

1. _____
2. _____
3. _____

I AM THANKFUL FOR...   DATE:
· ·

1. _____
2. _____
3. _____

I AM THANKFUL FOR...   DATE:
· ·

1. _____
2. _____
3. _____

I AM THANKFUL FOR...   DATE:
· ·

1. _____
2. _____
3. _____

I AM THANKFUL FOR...   DATE:
· ·

1. _____
2. _____
3. _____

Prayer:
_____
_____
_____

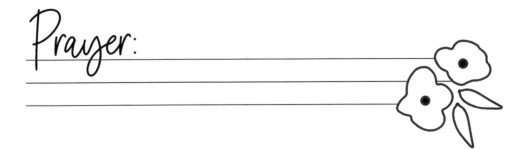

Give thanks to the Lord

For what you have done I will always praise you in the presence of your faithful people. And I will hope in your name, for your name is good.

Psalm 52:9

I AM THANKFUL FOR...   DATE:

1. _____
2. _____
3. _____

I AM THANKFUL FOR...   DATE:

1. _____
2. _____
3. _____

I AM THANKFUL FOR...   DATE:

1. _____
2. _____
3. _____

I AM THANKFUL FOR...   DATE:

1. _____
2. _____
3. _____

I AM THANKFUL FOR...   DATE:

1. _____
2. _____
3. _____

I AM THANKFUL FOR...   DATE:

1. _____
2. _____
3. _____

I AM THANKFUL FOR...   DATE:

1. _____
2. _____
3. _____

Prayer: _____

_____

Give thanks to the Lord

For everything God created is good, and nothing is to be rejected if it is received with thanksgiving, because it is consecrated by the word of God and prayer.

1 Timothy 4:4-5

I AM THANKFUL FOR...   DATE:

1. _____
2. _____
3. _____

I AM THANKFUL FOR...   DATE:

1. _____
2. _____
3. _____

I AM THANKFUL FOR...   DATE:

1. _____
2. _____
3. _____

I AM THANKFUL FOR...   DATE:

1. _____
2. _____
3. _____

I AM THANKFUL FOR...   DATE:

1. _____
2. _____
3. _____

I AM THANKFUL FOR...   DATE:

1. _____
2. _____
3. _____

I AM THANKFUL FOR...   DATE:

1. _____
2. _____
3. _____

Prayer: _____
_____
_____

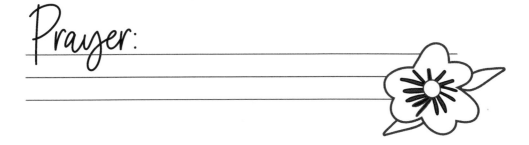

Give thanks to the Lord

Come, let us sing for joy to the LORD; let us shout aloud to the Rock of our salvation. Let us come before him with thanksgiving and extol him with music and song. For the LORD is the great God, the great King above all gods.

Psalm 95:1-3

I AM THANKFUL FOR...　　　DATE:

1.
2.
3.

I AM THANKFUL FOR...　　　DATE:

1.
2.
3.

I AM THANKFUL FOR...　　　DATE:

1.
2.
3.

I AM THANKFUL FOR...   DATE:
....

1. _____
2. _____
3. _____

I AM THANKFUL FOR...   DATE:
....

1. _____
2. _____
3. _____

I AM THANKFUL FOR...   DATE:
....

1. _____
2. _____
3. _____

I AM THANKFUL FOR...   DATE:
....

1. _____
2. _____
3. _____

Prayer: _____

_____

_____

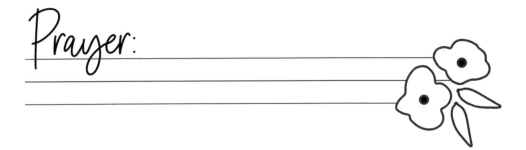

Give thanks to the Lord

> From them will come songs of thanksgiving and the sound of rejoicing. I will add to their numbers, and they will not be decreased; I will bring them honor, and they will not be disdained.
>
> Jeremiah 30:19

I AM THANKFUL FOR...   DATE:

1. _____
2. _____
3. _____

I AM THANKFUL FOR...   DATE:

1. _____
2. _____
3. _____

I AM THANKFUL FOR...   DATE:

1. _____
2. _____
3. _____

I AM THANKFUL FOR...   DATE:
....

1. _____
2. _____
3. _____

I AM THANKFUL FOR...   DATE:
....

1. _____
2. _____
3. _____

I AM THANKFUL FOR...   DATE:
....

1. _____
2. _____
3. _____

I AM THANKFUL FOR...   DATE:
....

1. _____
2. _____
3. _____

Prayer: _____

_____

_____

Give thanks to the Lord

The trumpeters and musicians joined in unison to give praise and thanks to the LORD. Accompanied by trumpets, cymbals and other instruments, the singers raised their voices in praise to the LORD and sang: "He is good; his love endures forever."

2 Chronicles 5:13

I AM THANKFUL FOR...   DATE:

1. _____
2. _____
3. _____

I AM THANKFUL FOR...   DATE:

1. _____
2. _____
3. _____

I AM THANKFUL FOR...   DATE:

1. _____
2. _____
3. _____

I AM THANKFUL FOR...   DATE:

1. _____
2. _____
3. _____

I AM THANKFUL FOR...   DATE:

1. _____
2. _____
3. _____

I AM THANKFUL FOR...   DATE:

1. _____
2. _____
3. _____

I AM THANKFUL FOR...   DATE:

1. _____
2. _____
3. _____

Prayer: _____
_____
_____

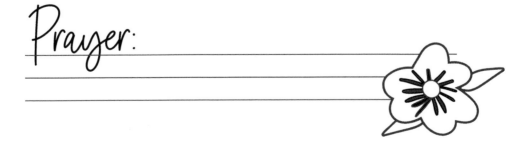

Give thanks to the Lord

Save us, LORD our God, and gather us from the nations, that we may give thanks to your holy name and glory in your praise.

Psalm 106:47

I AM THANKFUL FOR...   DATE:

1. _____
2. _____
3. _____

I AM THANKFUL FOR...   DATE:

1. _____
2. _____
3. _____

I AM THANKFUL FOR...   DATE:

1. _____
2. _____
3. _____

I AM THANKFUL FOR...   DATE:

1. _____
2. _____
3. _____

I AM THANKFUL FOR...   DATE:

1. _____
2. _____
3. _____

I AM THANKFUL FOR...   DATE:

1. _____
2. _____
3. _____

I AM THANKFUL FOR...   DATE:

1. _____
2. _____
3. _____

Prayer: _____

_____

_____

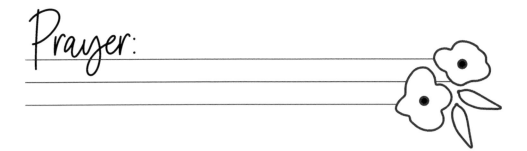

Give thanks to the Lord

Let the message of Christ dwell among you richly as you teach and admonish one another with all wisdom through psalms, hymns, and songs from the Spirit, singing to God with gratitude in your hearts.

Colossians 3:16

I AM THANKFUL FOR...   DATE:

1.

2.

3.

I AM THANKFUL FOR...   DATE:

1.

2.

3.

I AM THANKFUL FOR...   DATE:

1.

2.

3.

I AM THANKFUL FOR...   DATE:
....

1. _____
2. _____
3. _____

I AM THANKFUL FOR...   DATE:
....

1. _____
2. _____
3. _____

I AM THANKFUL FOR...   DATE:
....

1. _____
2. _____
3. _____

I AM THANKFUL FOR...   DATE:
....

1. _____
2. _____
3. _____

Prayer: _____

_____

_____

Give thanks to the Lord

Blessed be the God and Father of our Lord Jesus Christ, who has blessed us in Christ with every spiritual blessing in the heavenly places.

Ephesians 1:3

I AM THANKFUL FOR...   DATE:

1. _____
2. _____
3. _____

I AM THANKFUL FOR...   DATE:

1. _____
2. _____
3. _____

I AM THANKFUL FOR...   DATE:

1. _____
2. _____
3. _____

I AM THANKFUL FOR...   DATE:

1. _____
2. _____
3. _____

I AM THANKFUL FOR...   DATE:

1. _____
2. _____
3. _____

I AM THANKFUL FOR...   DATE:

1. _____
2. _____
3. _____

I AM THANKFUL FOR...   DATE:

1. _____
2. _____
3. _____

Prayer:
_____
_____
_____

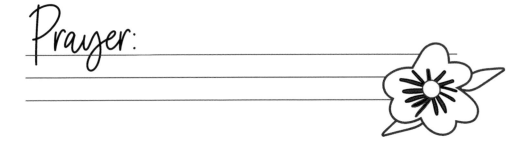

Give thanks to the Lord

> I will give you thanks in the great assembly;
> among the throngs I will praise you.
>
> Psalm 35:18

I AM THANKFUL FOR...   DATE:

1. _____
2. _____
3. _____

I AM THANKFUL FOR...   DATE:

1. _____
2. _____
3. _____

I AM THANKFUL FOR...   DATE:

1. _____
2. _____
3. _____

I AM THANKFUL FOR...   DATE:

1. _____
2. _____
3. _____

I AM THANKFUL FOR...   DATE:

1. _____
2. _____
3. _____

I AM THANKFUL FOR...   DATE:

1. _____
2. _____
3. _____

I AM THANKFUL FOR...   DATE:

1. _____
2. _____
3. _____

Prayer: _____
_____
_____

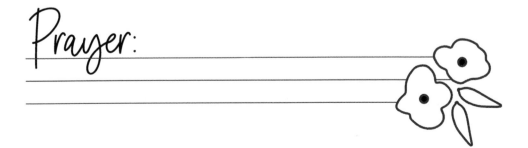

Give thanks to the Lord

> You will be enriched in every way so that you can be generous on every occasion, and through us your generosity will result in thanksgiving to God.
>
> 2 Corinthians 9:11

I AM THANKFUL FOR...   DATE:

1. _____
2. _____
3. _____

I AM THANKFUL FOR...   DATE:

1. _____
2. _____
3. _____

I AM THANKFUL FOR...   DATE:

1. _____
2. _____
3. _____

I AM THANKFUL FOR...   DATE:
. . . .

1. _____
2. _____
3. _____

I AM THANKFUL FOR...   DATE:
. . . .

1. _____
2. _____
3. _____

I AM THANKFUL FOR...   DATE:
. . . .

1. _____
2. _____
3. _____

I AM THANKFUL FOR...   DATE:
. . . .

1. _____
2. _____
3. _____

Prayer: _____

_____

_____

Give thanks to the Lord

And whatever you do, whether in word or deed, do it all in the name of the Lord Jesus, giving thanks to God the Father through him.

Colossians 3:17

I AM THANKFUL FOR...   DATE:

1.
2.
3.

I AM THANKFUL FOR...   DATE:

1.
2.
3.

I AM THANKFUL FOR...   DATE:

1.
2.
3.

I AM THANKFUL FOR...   DATE:

1. _____
2. _____
3. _____

I AM THANKFUL FOR...   DATE:

1. _____
2. _____
3. _____

I AM THANKFUL FOR...   DATE:

1. _____
2. _____
3. _____

I AM THANKFUL FOR...   DATE:

1. _____
2. _____
3. _____

Prayer: _____
_____
_____

prayers go up
blessings come down

Gratitude
CHECK IN

WRITE A PRAYER OF THANKSGIVING THANKING GOD
FOR HIS ABUNDANT GRACE AND MERCY. WHERE
CAN YOU GIVE YOURSELF A LITTLE MORE GRACE?

_____
_____
_____
_____
_____
_____
_____
_____
_____
_____
_____
_____
_____
_____
_____
_____
_____
_____
_____
_____
_____
_____
_____
_____

Give thanks to the Lord

The sounds of joy and gladness, the voices of bride and bridegroom, and the voices of those who bring thank offerings to the house of the LORD, saying, "Give thanks to the LORD Almighty, for the LORD is good; his love endures forever."
Jeremiah 33:11

I AM THANKFUL FOR...   DATE:

1.
2.
3.

I AM THANKFUL FOR...   DATE:

1.
2.
3.

I AM THANKFUL FOR...   DATE:

1.
2.
3.

I AM THANKFUL FOR...   DATE:
....

1. _____
2. _____
3. _____

I AM THANKFUL FOR...   DATE:
....

1. _____
2. _____
3. _____

I AM THANKFUL FOR...   DATE:
....

1. _____
2. _____
3. _____

I AM THANKFUL FOR...   DATE:
....

1. _____
2. _____
3. _____

Prayer: _____
_____
_____

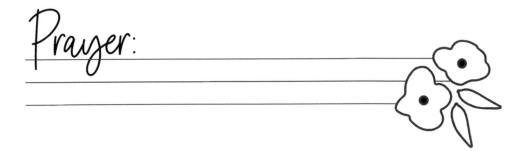

Give thanks to the Lord

> Give thanks to the LORD, for he is good; his love endures forever.
>
> Psalm 118:1

I AM THANKFUL FOR...   DATE:

1. _____
2. _____
3. _____

I AM THANKFUL FOR...   DATE:

1. _____
2. _____
3. _____

I AM THANKFUL FOR...   DATE:

1. _____
2. _____
3. _____

I AM THANKFUL FOR...   DATE:

1. _____
2. _____
3. _____

I AM THANKFUL FOR...   DATE:

1. _____
2. _____
3. _____

I AM THANKFUL FOR...   DATE:

1. _____
2. _____
3. _____

I AM THANKFUL FOR...   DATE:

1. _____
2. _____
3. _____

Prayer: _____
_____
_____

Give thanks to the Lord

Devote yourselves to prayer, being watchful and thankful.

Colossians 4:2

I AM THANKFUL FOR...   DATE:

1. _____
2. _____
3. _____

I AM THANKFUL FOR...   DATE:

1. _____
2. _____
3. _____

I AM THANKFUL FOR...   DATE:

1. _____
2. _____
3. _____

I AM THANKFUL FOR...   DATE:
....

1. _____

2. _____

3. _____

I AM THANKFUL FOR...   DATE:
....

1. _____

2. _____

3. _____

I AM THANKFUL FOR...   DATE:
....

1. _____

2. _____

3. _____

I AM THANKFUL FOR...   DATE:
....

1. _____

2. _____

3. _____

Prayer: _____

_____

_____

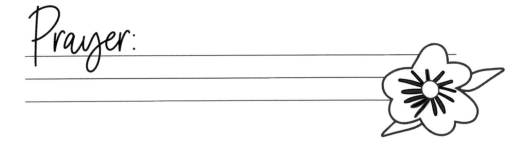

Give thanks to the Lord

Let them give thanks to the LORD for his unfailing love and his wonderful deeds for mankind. Let them sacrifice thank offerings and tell of his works with songs of joy.

Psalm 107:21-22

I AM THANKFUL FOR...   DATE:

1. _____
2. _____
3. _____

I AM THANKFUL FOR...   DATE:

1. _____
2. _____
3. _____

I AM THANKFUL FOR...   DATE:

1. _____
2. _____
3. _____

I AM THANKFUL FOR...   DATE:

1. _____
2. _____
3. _____

I AM THANKFUL FOR...   DATE:

1. _____
2. _____
3. _____

I AM THANKFUL FOR...   DATE:

1. _____
2. _____
3. _____

I AM THANKFUL FOR...   DATE:

1. _____
2. _____
3. _____

Prayer: _____
_____
_____

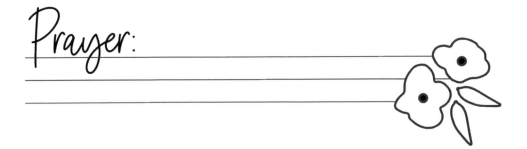

Give thanks to the Lord

I will praise God's name in song and glorify him with thanksgiving.

Psalm 69:30

I AM THANKFUL FOR...　　　　DATE:

1. _____
2. _____
3. _____

I AM THANKFUL FOR...　　　　DATE:

1. _____
2. _____
3. _____

I AM THANKFUL FOR...　　　　DATE:

1. _____
2. _____
3. _____

I AM THANKFUL FOR...   DATE:

1. _____
2. _____
3. _____

I AM THANKFUL FOR...   DATE:

1. _____
2. _____
3. _____

I AM THANKFUL FOR...   DATE:

1. _____
2. _____
3. _____

I AM THANKFUL FOR...   DATE:

1. _____
2. _____
3. _____

Prayer: _____

_____

_____

Give thanks to the Lord

Thanks be to God for his inexpressible gift!

2 Corinthians 9:15

I AM THANKFUL FOR...   DATE:
....

1. _____

2. _____

3. _____

I AM THANKFUL FOR...   DATE:
....

1. _____

2. _____

3. _____

I AM THANKFUL FOR...   DATE:
....

1. _____

2. _____

3. _____

I AM THANKFUL FOR...   DATE:
....

1. _____
2. _____
3. _____

I AM THANKFUL FOR...   DATE:
....

1. _____
2. _____
3. _____

I AM THANKFUL FOR...   DATE:
....

1. _____
2. _____
3. _____

I AM THANKFUL FOR...   DATE:
....

1. _____
2. _____
3. _____

Prayer: _____

_____

_____

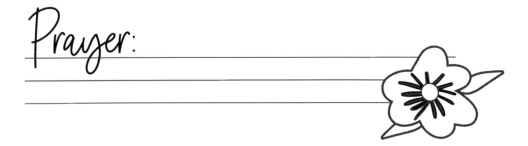

Give thanks to the Lord

> Jesus then took the loaves, gave thanks, and distributed to those who were seated as much as they wanted. He did the same with the fish.
>
> John 6:11

I AM THANKFUL FOR...   DATE:

1. _____
2. _____
3. _____

I AM THANKFUL FOR...   DATE:

1. _____
2. _____
3. _____

I AM THANKFUL FOR...   DATE:

1. _____
2. _____
3. _____

I AM THANKFUL FOR...   DATE:
....

1. _____
2. _____
3. _____

I AM THANKFUL FOR...   DATE:
....

1. _____
2. _____
3. _____

I AM THANKFUL FOR...   DATE:
....

1. _____
2. _____
3. _____

I AM THANKFUL FOR...   DATE:
....

1. _____
2. _____
3. _____

Prayer: _____

_____

_____

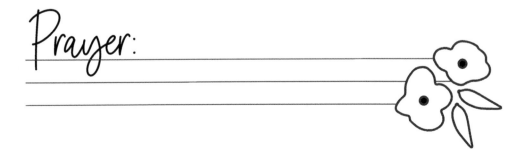

Give thanks to the Lord

And now we thank you, our God, and praise your glorious name.

1 Chronicles 29:13

I AM THANKFUL FOR...   DATE:

1. _____

2. _____

3. _____

I AM THANKFUL FOR...   DATE:

1. _____

2. _____

3. _____

I AM THANKFUL FOR...   DATE:

1. _____

2. _____

3. _____

I AM THANKFUL FOR...   DATE:
....

1. _____
2. _____
3. _____

I AM THANKFUL FOR...   DATE:
....

1. _____
2. _____
3. _____

I AM THANKFUL FOR...   DATE:
....

1. _____
2. _____
3. _____

I AM THANKFUL FOR...   DATE:
....

1. _____
2. _____
3. _____

Prayer: _____

_____

Give thanks to the Lord

But I with the voice of thanksgiving will sacrifice to you; what I have vowed I will pay. Salvation belongs to the LORD!

Jonah 2:9

I AM THANKFUL FOR...   DATE:

1. _____
2. _____
3. _____

I AM THANKFUL FOR...   DATE:

1. _____
2. _____
3. _____

I AM THANKFUL FOR...   DATE:

1. _____
2. _____
3. _____

I AM THANKFUL FOR...   DATE:

1. _____
2. _____
3. _____

I AM THANKFUL FOR...   DATE:

1. _____
2. _____
3. _____

I AM THANKFUL FOR...   DATE:

1. _____
2. _____
3. _____

I AM THANKFUL FOR...   DATE:

1. _____
2. _____
3. _____

Prayer: _____

_____

_____

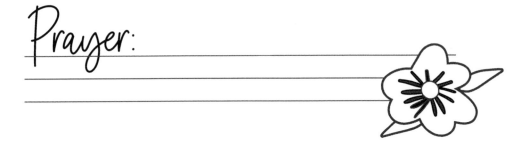

Give thanks to the Lord

> But thanks be to God, who in Christ always leads us in triumphal procession, and through us spreads the fragrance of the knowledge of him everywhere.
>
> 2 Corinthians 2:14

I AM THANKFUL FOR...   DATE:

1. _____
2. _____
3. _____

I AM THANKFUL FOR...   DATE:

1. _____
2. _____
3. _____

I AM THANKFUL FOR...   DATE:

1. _____
2. _____
3. _____

I AM THANKFUL FOR...   DATE:

1. _____
2. _____
3. _____

I AM THANKFUL FOR...   DATE:

1. _____
2. _____
3. _____

I AM THANKFUL FOR...   DATE:

1. _____
2. _____
3. _____

I AM THANKFUL FOR...   DATE:

1. _____
2. _____
3. _____

Prayer: _____
_____
_____

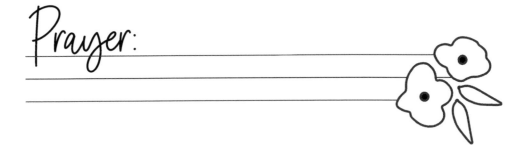

Give thanks to the Lord

> I will praise you, Lord my God, with all my heart; I will glorify your name forever.
>
> Psalm 86:12

I AM THANKFUL FOR...   DATE:

1. _____
2. _____
3. _____

I AM THANKFUL FOR...   DATE:

1. _____
2. _____
3. _____

I AM THANKFUL FOR...   DATE:

1. _____
2. _____
3. _____

I AM THANKFUL FOR...   DATE:
....

1. _____
2. _____
3. _____

I AM THANKFUL FOR...   DATE:
....

1. _____
2. _____
3. _____

I AM THANKFUL FOR...   DATE:
....

1. _____
2. _____
3. _____

I AM THANKFUL FOR...   DATE:
....

1. _____
2. _____
3. _____

Prayer: _____

_____

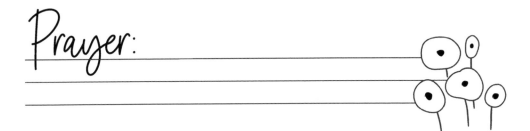

Give thanks to the Lord

And God is able to bless you abundantly, so that in all things at all times, having all that you need, you will abound in every good work.

2 Corinthians 9:8

I AM THANKFUL FOR...   DATE:

1. _____
2. _____
3. _____

I AM THANKFUL FOR...   DATE:

1. _____
2. _____
3. _____

I AM THANKFUL FOR...   DATE:

1. _____
2. _____
3. _____

I AM THANKFUL FOR...   DATE:

1.
2.
3.

I AM THANKFUL FOR...   DATE:

1.
2.
3.

I AM THANKFUL FOR...   DATE:

1.
2.
3.

I AM THANKFUL FOR...   DATE:

1.
2.
3.

Prayer:

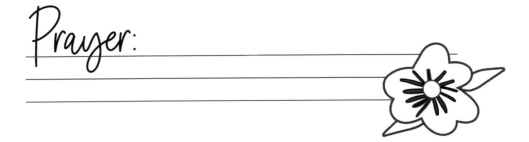

Give thanks to the Lord

The Lord bless you and keep you; the Lord make his face to shine upon you and be gracious to you; the Lord lift up his countenance upon you and give you peace.

Numbers 6:24-26

I AM THANKFUL FOR...   DATE:

1. _____
2. _____
3. _____

I AM THANKFUL FOR...   DATE:

1. _____
2. _____
3. _____

I AM THANKFUL FOR...   DATE:

1. _____
2. _____
3. _____

I AM THANKFUL FOR...   DATE:

1. _____
2. _____
3. _____

I AM THANKFUL FOR...   DATE:

1. _____
2. _____
3. _____

I AM THANKFUL FOR...   DATE:

1. _____
2. _____
3. _____

I AM THANKFUL FOR...   DATE:

1. _____
2. _____
3. _____

Prayer: _____
_____
_____

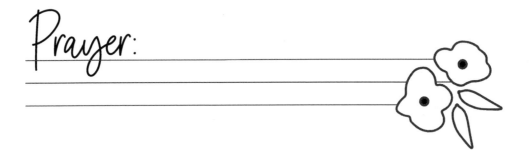

focus your heart on what
really matters

Gratitude

CHECK IN

WRITE A PRAYER THANKING GOD THAT OUR IDENTITY IS IN
HIM ALONE. THANK HIM FOR THE WAYS HE HAS TRANSFORMED
YOUR HEART AND HOW HE CAN CONTINUE TO DO SO.

_____

_____

_____

_____

_____

_____

_____

_____

_____

_____

_____

_____

_____

_____

_____

_____

_____

_____

_____

_____

_____

_____

Made in the USA
Columbia, SC
19 December 2019